More Than Enough

SANDRA D. RHOADS

WestBow Press books may be ordered through booksellers or by contacting:

WestBow Press
A Division of Thomas Nelson & Zondervan
1663 Liberty Drive
Bloomington, IN 47403
www.westbowpress.com
844-714-3454

Because of the dynamic nature of the Internet, any web addresses or links contained in
this book may have changed since publication and may no longer be valid. The views
expressed in this work are solely those of the author and do not necessarily reflect the views
of the publisher, and the publisher hereby disclaims any responsibility for them.

Any people depicted in stock imagery provided by Getty Images are models,
and such images are being used for illustrative purposes only.
Certain stock imagery © Getty Images.

ISBN: 979-8-3850-1232-9(sc)
ISBN: 979-8-3850-1233-6 (hc)
ISBN: 979-8-3850-1231-2 (e)

Library of Congress Control Number: 2023921698

Print information available on the last page.

WestBow Press rev. date: 11/28/2023

WESTBOW
PRESS®
A DIVISION OF THOMAS NELSON
& ZONDERVAN

More Than Enough

More than Enough

Callie is a spunky, petite, freckled-faced girl with red curly hair. She is as cute as a button and has a personality that could light up a room. Her laugh is contagious, and she is mature beyond her eight years. Callie loves to sing, dance, and play the piano. She also plays soccer, softball, hide-and-seek, and miniature golf. When wearing pants, no one notices Callie has a prosthetic leg. Callie has learned to do whatever kids her age or older can do. The belief that when you have God in your life you have more than enough has been engrained in her by her parents. Her parents, teachers, and coaches always encourage her to have faith and a can-do attitude. With a positive attitude, faith, and perseverance, Callie does not let her disability hinder her from doing whatever she attempts or is able to do. Despite her disability, she believes God has blessed her and will continue to bless her with more than enough to be happy and successful in life.

Every night since the day they adopted Callie at birth, her mother or father reads a bedtime story to her. After story time and a prayer, her mother will say, "Callie, always remember God has great plans for your life. He has blessed you with more than enough to carry out His plans. He will use you to do wonderful things! You are smart, talented, creative, loving, and friendly. You are beautiful inside and out. Your father and I love you more than there are stars in the sky, more than there are grains of sand on all the beaches, and more than there are blades of grass on all the earth."

Then Callie replies, "I love you too!"

Her daddy says, "I love you more. But God loves you most! Now, go to Sleepy-Town!" Callie is the apple of their eyes.

4

Every month—on holidays, birthdays, or out of the blue—Callie's father will bring her mother flowers, dance around the room with her mother, and sing the song "Misty" to her. Callie never asks why he does that. She just listens to the words to the song and figures it out. She knows her daddy is so happy and filled with love and appreciation for her mother that it brings tears of joy to his eyes. Callie claps and giggles watching them. He also brings a little bouquet to Callie, twirls her around the room and sings "You Are So Beautiful." Callie and her mother beam with joy! This makes Callie and her mother feel treasured and so very special!

One day Callie and her father go to the store for ice cream. Her favorite flavor is strawberry. Callie notices a flyer with a picture on it taped to the store window. It reads, "Free Boston Terrier puppy to a loving home, 8 weeks old, has all required shots, call 888-4487." Immediately, with urgency, and pointing to the sign, Callie says, "Daddy, Daddy, look! Can we get him? He's so cute! Can we go get him before someone else gets him? Can we, Daddy? Can we?"

Her father replies, "Callie, a puppy is a big responsibility. You must feed him, take him out to potty, clean up after him, train him, walk him, play with him, and show him lots of love. You have school, your sports, piano lessons, and chores. Can you do all of that and take care of a puppy too?"

"Yes, Daddy, but I might need a little help sometimes," she replies.

"Well, we will have to talk it over with your mother," he responds. Callie's father takes a picture of the flyer on his cell phone. Callie can hardly wait to get home to persuade her mother.

When they get home, Callie runs into the house yelling, "Mommy, Mommy, can we get a puppy? He's so cute, and he's free! I will take care of him, and love him, and do everything I am supposed to do. I promise! Can I, Mommy? Can I?"

"May I?" says her mother, correcting Callie's grammar.

"May I?" Callie repeats with the same enthusiasm. Her daddy explains they saw the flyer in the store window and shows her mother the picture on his cell phone. Her mother reinforces to Callie that a puppy is a big responsibility, requiring a lot of time and work. Callie insists she is prepared to do it. She points out that their fenced backyard has lots of room for the puppy to run and play. Callie has proven herself to be very good at doing her chores around the house, doing her school homework, and practicing her piano lessons. So, her mother agrees to go see the puppy. Callie's father calls the number on the flyer and arranges to go see the puppy the next day.

That night, Callie prays and asks God to keep this puppy for her, and the puppy will like her. She cannot go to sleep because she is thinking about all the things she will teach the puppy—like sit, stay, up, lay down, and rollover. She imagines the games they will play, like hide-and-seek, catch, tug-of-war, and fetch. She wonders what she will name him, and what kind of puppy food he will like. Callie makes a list in her head of all the things they will need to buy for the puppy. She hopes she remembers to take a towel with her to lay in her lap when they get the puppy—in case he has an accident in the car. She reminds herself quietly, "Don't forget a leash." She does not want him to wander off. Callie loves that puppy already! All of this thinking, and remembering, and planning exhausts her, and she finally falls asleep.

The next day, on their way to the home where the puppy is, Callie cannot stop talking about what she is going to name the puppy, where the puppy will sleep, and what tricks she will teach him. When they arrive at the location, the owner escorts them to the fenced backyard where the puppy is playing. Immediately, the puppy runs to Callie, toppling over as he runs. Callie kneels down, and the puppy jumps into her arms and licks all over her face. "He's giving me kisses," Callie squeals! Callie does not notice that the puppy has three normal legs and one front leg shorter than the others. She just sees the puppy has lots of love to give. The owner tells them that many people have come by to see the puppy, but no one wanted the puppy because she is not perfect.

"It's a *girl*! She's perfect for me! God saved her for me! May I keep her?" Callie exclaims. She looks at her parents while holding the puppy tight as it wiggles and kisses her. "I will name her Misty," Callie announces, without waiting for an answer.

Her mom and dad look at each other and laugh. Her dad responds, "Well, I guess we have adopted a puppy!" They thank the owner of the puppy for this precious gift and assure him they will take good care of Misty. Then they proceed to the pet store to buy a leash, kennel, dog bed, squeaky toys, puppy supplies, and puppy food for Misty. Callie has a great time helping pick out stuff for Misty. That night Misty sleeps on Callie's bed. This is no surprise to her parents.

Month after month, Callie keeps her promise and takes Misty for walks, out to potty, feeds her, plays with her in her free time, picks up after Misty, and teaches her tricks. Showing her lots of love is easy. But her mom and dad often help Callie with the puppy. Callie's mother works from home, so she takes care of Misty while Callie is in school. Misty is a wonderful addition to their family. Every night after story time when her mother or father have left her bedroom, Callie hugs Misty and quietly tells her something like, "I love you more than I can count, more than all the words in the dictionary, more than all the hairs on everyone's heads, more than all the leaves on all the trees." Of course, most nights, Callie thinks of something different to compare her love to. Misty kisses her all over her face, and Callie giggles with delight. Some nights they are so loud, her mom or dad comes back into Callie's bedroom. They say sternly, "Go to Sleepy-Town you two!"

Every morning before she leaves for school, Callie kisses Misty. She says, "I love you!" and, "I'll be back! Be a good girl!" Every school day at three-thirty Misty waits by the door with a leash in her mouth for Callie to return. It is as though Misty has a built-in alarm clock. Misty just seems to know when it is time for Callie to return home from school. Callie will come through the door, and Misty will bark with glee! Callie will kneel down, and Misty will jump up on Callie, licking her with kisses. Then Misty will pick up her leash again in anticipation of taking a walk with Callie. "Let's go see what's happening in the neighborhood, Misty," Callie says eagerly!

One night there is a terrible thunderstorm with lots of powerful lightning. Misty is asleep in her bed on the floor by Callie's bed. Suddenly Misty awakens and starts barking furiously, jumping up and down. Callie does not know what to make of it. She hastily gets out of bed and goes to her parents' bedroom, with Misty trailing behind and barking continuously. Callie tells them something is wrong with Misty. Misty runs back to the hallway, barking, jumping up and down, and looking up toward the attic. Callie's father jumps out of bed, swiftly goes to the hallway and inquires, "What's up there, Misty?" Looking up toward the attic, Misty keeps barking intensely. Callie's dad goes up the attic stairs, opens the door, and notices flames in the attic ceiling! Lightning has struck the roof! He swiftly comes down the stairs and tells everyone to hurry outside. Callie swoops up Misty and immediately does what she is told. Her mom and dad follow right behind them.

Once outside, Callie, Misty, and Callie's parents wait across the street from their house. Callie's dad immediately telephones the fire department. The firemen come quickly and put the fire out. Callie's father tells the fire chief how Misty woke the family and alerted them of danger from the smoke in the attic. The fire chief informs them that there is not a lot of damage, thanks to Misty's keen sense of smell, and her warning them of impending danger. Hugging and kissing Misty, Callie exclaims, "God used you to save our lives, Misty! You're my hero! We love you, Misty! You may not have everything you're supposed to have, but just like me, God gave you more than enough of lots of other amazing things!"

Printed in the United States
by Baker & Taylor Publisher Services